D1523171

THE SCIENCE OF
HURRICANES

ANGELA ROYSTON

Gareth Stevens
Publishing

Please visit our website, www.garethstevens.com. For a free color catalog of all our high-quality books, call toll free 1-800-542-2595 or fax 1-877-542-2596.

Library of Congress Cataloging-in-Publication Data

Royston, Angela, 1945-
 The science of hurricanes / Angela Royston.
    p. cm. — (Nature's wrath)
 Includes index.
ISBN 978-1-4339-8660-4 (pbk.)
ISBN 978-1-4339-8661-1 (6-pack)
ISBN 978-1-4339-8659-8 (library binding)
1. Hurricanes—Juvenile literature. I. Title. II. Series: Nature's wrath.
 QC944.R69 2013
 551.55'2—dc23

2012037758

First Edition

Published in 2013 by
Gareth Stevens Publishing
111 East 14th Street, Suite 349
New York, NY 10003

© 2013 Gareth Stevens Publishing

Produced by Calcium, www.calciumcreative.co.uk
Designed by Simon Borrough and Nick Leggett
Edited by Sarah Eason and Robyn Hardyman
Picture research by Susannah Jayes

Photo credits: Cover: Top: Shutterstock: Neo Edmund; Bottom (l to r): Dreamstime: Dreammediapeel; Shutterstock: Olga Lipatova, Photobank.kiev.ua, Marc van Vuren, Gary Yim. Inside: Dreamstime: Bhikshuni 15bl, Chhobi 23b, Conde 1c, 12c, Alan Crosthwaite 32tr, Dmcdesign 16–17tc, 28c, 45l, Shannon Drawe 13b, Steven Frame 22r, Giromin 20cl, Brian Grant 20tr, Isselee 34cr, Remy Levine 33l, Dario Martin 14tr, Federico Montemurro 28–29c, Terry Poche 10cr, Sk8bette 44cr, David Snyder 40–41c, 42tr, 42cr, 43tr, Vesilvio 9t; FEMA Photo: Leif Skoogfors 7; NASA: Earth Sciences & Image Analysis Laboratory/Mike Trenchard 8c; NOAA: 21; Shutterstock: B747 4c, Tad Denson 24c, 26tr, Vladislav Gurfinkel 19, Gina Jacobs 17cl, Caitlin Mirra 1b, 11b, 30r, 34tr, 35cl, Tomislav Pinter 31c, SeanPavonePhoto 15cl, Stacie Stauff Smith Photography 25b; US Marine Corps: Sgt. Ezekiel R. Kitandwe 27; Wikipedia: Staff Sergeant Val Gempis (USAF) 5t, NASA/Nilfanion 6tr, TAFB/NHC/NOAA 18tr.

Printed in the United States of America

CPSIA compliance information: Batch #CW13GS: For further information contact Gareth Stevens, New York, New York at 1-800-542-2595.

CONTENTS

WHAT IS A HURRICANE?

A hurricane is a severe tropical storm. Hurricanes are large, typically several hundred miles wide. They build up far out at sea. Howling winds sweep across the ocean, stirring up huge waves. When they hit land, they pound the coast. Hurricane winds are loud—survivors have said they sound like a freight train rolling down the street. With the wind comes very heavy rain. Together they are devastating. Around 40 to 50 hurricanes strike land somewhere around the world each year.

Damage from Wind and Water

Hurricane winds can pull trees and other plants out of the ground. They can also overturn cars, trucks, and mobile homes. They can lift off roofs and even destroy people's houses. They send signs and billboards flying through the air and bring down telephone lines. The torrential rains cause even more destruction. Drains, gutters, streams, and rivers flood. Seawater crashes over the shore in a storm surge. It pours into streets and onto fields, washing everything away.

Strong winds and heavy rain battered palm trees in Florida during this hurricane. Palm trees usually survive a hurricane, because their trunks bend with the wind.

4

In 1991, Cyclone Marian hit the southeast coast of Bangladesh in southern Asia. The land was flooded by water from the river and the sea. Homes and farmland were destroyed.

Hurricane, Cyclone, and Typhoon

Hurricane, *cyclone*, and *typhoon* are all different names for the same event. In the Caribbean and North America, a severe tropical storm is called a hurricane. In China, Japan, and eastern Asia it is called a typhoon, and in the Indian Ocean and Australia it is called a cyclone.

In 1970, a cyclone hit the island of Bhola and other islands and land in the huge delta of the River Ganges, in East Pakistan (now Bangladesh) and India. No one knows exactly how many people were killed, but the number is estimated to be between 300,000 and 500,000. It is the deadliest hurricane on record.

CHAPTER ONE

THE INSIDE STORY

Tropical storms form over warm seas near the equator. As the storm strengthens, the wind begins to circle around a still center, called the eye. The whole storm moves across the ocean, away from the equator. In the Northern Hemisphere, storms move toward the northwest, and in the Southern Hemisphere, toward the south and southwest.

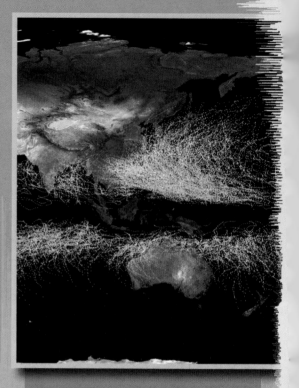

This map of Asia and Australia shows the paths of each recorded hurricane, cyclone, and typhoon between 1985 and 2005. The blue dots on each path were plotted every 6 hours.

STORM SEASON

Tropical storms are common in different regions at different times of the year. Hurricanes are most likely to hit the Caribbean, Central America, and Florida from June through November. Typhoons batter the Philippines, China, and Japan and cyclones pound Bangladesh, Burma, and Pakistan from April through December. Cyclones hit Australia and Madagascar from November through April. Each region of the world has an alphabetical list of names it uses for hurricanes. The first major storm of the season has a name beginning with "A," then the second name begins with "B," and so on.

WORLD'S WORST

The worst season for hurricanes ever recorded was in 2005, when 12 major hurricanes hit the Caribbean, Mexico, and the United States. Hurricane Wilma was the 23rd named tropical storm that season and the most intense hurricane ever recorded in the region.

These are just a few of the many homes damaged by Hurricane Wilma when it hit Cancun, Mexico, in 2005. The houses are built on stilts, but that did not protect them from the full force of the hurricane's power.

A HURRICANE FORMS

A hurricane begins as a thunderstorm that forms over warm ocean waters. The temperature at the surface must be at least 80°F (26.5°C). Most Atlantic hurricanes begin as a series of thunderstorms off the west coast of Africa. Hot, damp air from the surface of the ocean rises into the storm. As the air rises, cooler air from the surrounding area moves in to replace it. This cooler air is wind. If the storm crosses a large area of rising, damp air, it pulls in more cool air and the winds become stronger.

A satellite took this photograph of a hurricane. It shows the eye at the center and huge clouds of wind and rain spiraling around it.

eye

Spiraling Winds

As the storm travels across the ocean, it picks up more moist air. Wind speeds increase as air is sucked in. The spin of the earth causes the winds in the storm to spiral around the center. When the winds reach 74 miles (119 km) per hour, the storm has become a hurricane. It can take hours or several days for the storm to develop into a hurricane.

WORLD'S WORST

Typhoon Tip was the largest tropical cyclone ever recorded. It measured 1,380 miles (2,220 km) across. It moved up through the western Pacific Ocean and hit the coast of Japan on October 17, 1979.

Inside a Hurricane

A hurricane can measure 100 miles (160 km) or more across. The eye is at the center of the hurricane. It is an area of calm, with only light wind and blue sky. Around the eye is the eye wall. This belt of thick cloud is the part with the heaviest rain. The strongest winds are just outside the eye wall. The winds become weaker toward the outer edge of the hurricane.

These storm clouds are in the eye wall at the center of a hurricane. Here, the wind is strongest, and the rain is heaviest. The wild weather in the eye wall often produces thunderstorms and tornadoes.

HURRICANES ON THE MOVE

A hurricane changes as it moves across the ocean. It becomes stronger when it moves over warmer water and weaker when it moves across cooler water. The strength of a hurricane is measured by the speed of its winds. A hurricane's strength is categorized according to the Saffir-Simpson Scale.

Power lines in Louisiana were blown down when Hurricane Gustav struck the state as a Category 2 hurricane in 2008. Loss of electricity and water supply is very common following a hurricane.

Measuring Hurricanes

The Saffir-Simpson Scale was created to measure hurricanes around North and South America. Today, it is also used to measure cyclones and typhoons.

This table shows the categories used to measure hurricanes.

Category	Wind Speed	Examples of Damage
1 Minimal	74–95 mph (119–153 kph)	Damage to trees and shrubs.
2 Moderate	96–110 mph (154–177 kph)	Damage to roofs and mobile homes; trees blown down; flooding on the coast.
3 Extensive	111–130 mph (178–209 kph)	Much damage to buildings; buildings near the coast could be flooded.
4 Extreme	131–155 mph (210–249 kph)	Much damage to buildings; buildings near the coast could be flooded.
5 Catastrophic	over 155 mph (over 250 kph)	Large buildings badly damaged; major flooding.

From Sea to Land

When a hurricane crosses the ocean to land, it is said to make "landfall." The winds get their energy from the warm sea, so they quickly lose their power over a large area of land. Three hurricanes classified as Category 5 have made landfall on the United States. The winds they brought were more than double the speed limit for vehicles on the freeway!

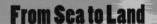
Winds of 190 miles (310 km) per hour hit the Florida Keys in 1935, and the Mississippi coast in 1969. More recently, in 1992, Hurricane Andrew hit Florida with winds of 175 miles (280 km) per hour.

This street in New Orleans was flooded in 2005 after Hurricane Katrina made landfall as a Category 3 hurricane.

SURGING ONTO THE SHORE

As a hurricane gets close to land, its strong winds push huge amounts of seawater onto the shore. This is called a storm surge. A storm surge hits the coast before the main force of the hurricane arrives. A Category 5 hurricane can produce a storm surge of more than 20 feet (6 m).

Huge waves battered the sea wall in Havana, Cuba, during this hurricane, threatening buildings along the seafront.

Storm Tides

The level of the sea at the shore rises and falls naturally twice a day, producing two high tides and two low tides. A storm tide is the combination of a storm surge with a natural high tide. As a result, storm tides produce a higher rise in sea level than a high tide or a storm surge would on their own.

Shape of the Beach

The height of a storm surge and the amount of damage it causes on land depends on the shape of the beach as well as on the strength of the wind. If the beach has a shallow slope, the storm surge will be much higher than on a beach with a steep slope. This is because on a shallow slope, the waters have a longer area over which to gain height.

Boats were swept onto the land on Galveston Island, Texas, during Hurricane Ike in 2008. Marinas and harbors can be badly damaged by storm surges.

REAL-LIFE SCIENCE
HURRICANE IRENE,
Atlantic Ocean, 2011

Hurricane Irene was a very large hurricane that caused heavy rainfall and flooding along its path. It measured 510 miles (820 km) across and traveled from the Caribbean along the East Coast of the United States and into Canada. At its height it was a Category 3 hurricane, but even when it weakened to a tropical storm it still caused great damage.

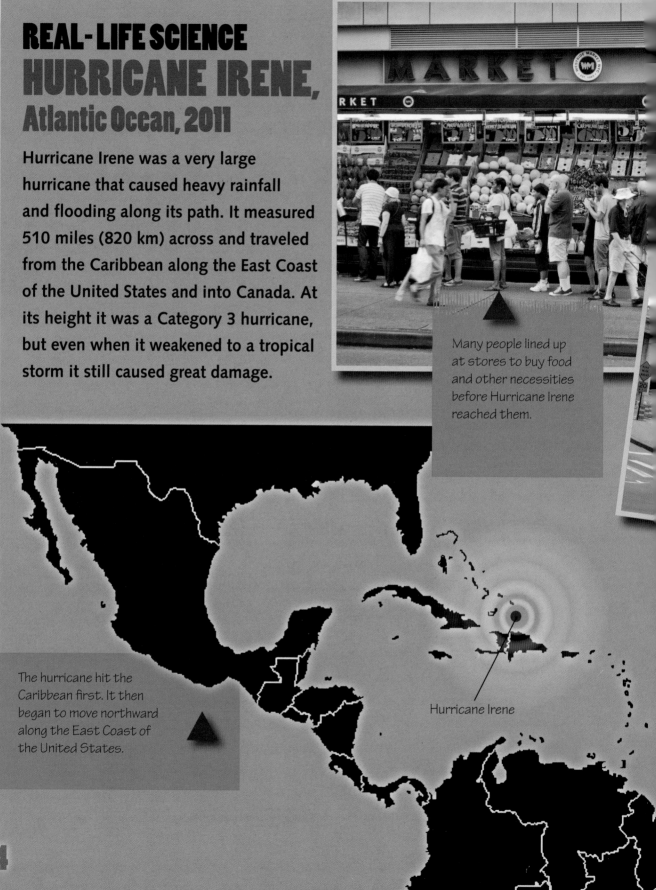

Many people lined up at stores to buy food and other necessities before Hurricane Irene reached them.

The hurricane hit the Caribbean first. It then began to move northward along the East Coast of the United States.

Hurricane Irene

Residents on the coast near New York were ordered to move inland before Hurricane Irene struck. This sign warns motorists not to drive down to that area.

Stores and offices closed to prepare for the coming hurricane hit.

India Hicks lives on Harbor Island, a tiny island in the Bahamas:

"The sea was raging. The windows, walls, and doors began to scream. Irene had arrived. In the early hours of the following morning, the winds dropped, and a strange calm spread across the island. The eye was over us, so we went outside. The beach was a mess—all the steps had been shredded, every cabaña was missing. The skies darkened once again, and we hurried back to the house."

From Puerto Rico to the Bahamas

Hurricane Irene was the ninth named tropical storm and the first major hurricane of 2011. It began as a tropical storm in the Atlantic Ocean during August, and strengthened to a hurricane as it moved across Puerto Rico and along the north coast of the Dominican Republic. Here, the coast was continually lashed by strong winds and heavy waves.

The hurricane strengthened to Category 3 on August 24, as it passed over the warm waters of the Bahamas. It destroyed 100 homes on the eastern islands of the Bahamas and brought down trees and power lines. Up to 13 inches (33 cm) of rain fell in some places.

15

MOVING NORTH

Hurricane Irene headed north from the Bahamas, sparing Florida. Nevertheless, 65 million people who lived on the Eastern Seaboard were in its pathway. The hurricane swept up the coast, moving from the ocean to the land three times. It made landfall near Cape Lookout in North Carolina on August 27, and near Brigantine Island, New Jersey, and near New York City on August 28.

Flooding and Power Cuts

As the hurricane left the tropical waters, it lost energy. Its wind speed dropped below 74 miles (120 km) per hour, and it became a tropical storm. Nevertheless, heavy rain caused flooding inland and on the coast, while waves up to 9 feet (2.7 m) high battered the shore. Floods blocked highways, and the wind uprooted trees and blew down power lines. More than 7 million homes and businesses lost power, which took several days to repair. Hurricane Irene claimed 56 lives, and the damage it caused cost more than $18 billion to repair.

Even after the hurricane had passed, it continued to cause destruction and havoc. On August 28, the Pomperaug River in Connecticut flooded onto farmland and into homes in Southbury.

The Story of Hurricane Irene

AUG 20, 2011
A tropical storm around 190 miles (305 km) east of the Lesser Antilles islands in the Caribbean is given the name Irene.

AUG 21, 2011
Irene heads toward the US Virgin Islands

and Puerto Rico. The residents on the islands begin to prepare for the hurricane ahead.

AUG 22, 2011
Irene strengthens and makes landfall on the east coast of Puerto Rico as a

Category 1 hurricane. Meteorologists watch to see the path that the hurricane will take next.

AUG 23, 2011
Irene moves northwest along the north coast of the Dominican Republic

as a Category 2 hurricane. The coastline of the island is battered by the storm's winds and lashing waves.

AUG 24 , 2011
Next, Irene batters the Turks and Caicos Islands. As the

This neighborhood was flooded when the nearby river burst its banks. Some people were rescued by boat, while others waded to dry land carrying their pets and most important possessions.

Laurie Lande and her husband were staying just north of New York City when Hurricane Irene struck the coast:

"We were glued to the news coverage as the hurricane made its way up the coast. Just after midnight the power went out. Flashlights in hand, we went to bed as the wind howled. The rain continued off and on next day. After the power went out, the water was next. And no running water meant no working toilets. There was a sense of total isolation. There was no phone service, no television, and very spotty cell phone reception."

hurricane moves over the very warm waters of the Bahamas, it increases in size and strength, and quickly becomes a Category 3 hurricane.

AUG 25–26, 2011
Irene weakens as it heads for the US East Coast, and approaches North Carolina as a Category 1 hurricane.

AUG 27, 2011 7:30 a.m.
Irene makes landfall in North Carolina and moves over land for around 10 hours, before moving back over the Atlantic near Chesapeake Bay in Virginia.

AUG 28, 2011 5:35 a.m.
Irene weakens to a tropical storm and makes landfall in New Jersey, before moving over the ocean and northeast, hugging the New Jersey coast.

AUG 28 , 2011 9:00 a.m.
Irene makes landfall near New York City, then moves northeast over New England into Canada.

CHAPTER TWO

GETTING READY

A hurricane unleashes huge forces that can kill and injure people and damage buildings, trees, power lines, boats, and other vehicles. Scientists cannot prevent hurricanes from happening, but they can warn people when a hurricane is forming and work out the path it is likely to take. This gives locals time to protect themselves and their property.

These are the offices of the National Hurricane Center where meteorologists study tropical storms. The office is quiet in this photograph, but when a hurricane is brewing it buzzes with activity.

PREPARING FOR A HURRICANE

Meteorologists are scientists who study the weather. A Cuban priest named Father Benito Viñes was the first meteorologist to observe the clouds that build up before a hurricane arrives. In the 1870s, he set up observation posts, which helped him to accurately predict the path of approaching hurricanes. He was able to warn people not only in Cuba, but in Puerto Rico, the Bahamas, and other islands, too.

FIRST WARNINGS

Father Benito Viñes's first recorded hurricane prediction was printed on September 11, 1875. It saved the lives of many Cubans by warning them of a violent hurricane that hit the south coast of the island 2 days later.

National Hurricane Center

After Father Viñes died in 1893, the United States Signal Corps and then the Weather Bureau took over his work. The National Hurricane Center was formed in 1956. It is still the organization that monitors hurricanes and issues warnings for the United States. Today, governments in many countries also educate people about hurricanes, so they know how to keep safe when one strikes.

Meteorologists track the path of a hurricane using satellite images. They study the progression of the hurricane to predict how the storm will develop and where it will hit.

TRACKING THE STORMS

Meteorologists use technology and science to identify and track storms and hurricanes. Weather satellites that orbit Earth take photographs of the clouds, land, and sea below. Scientists monitor the photos on their computers and look out for tropical storms. Specially equipped aircraft are also used to gather data about hurricanes that may be developing out in the ocean. With all this information, scientists can even build up a picture of the whole upcoming season, and how many hurricanes it is likely to produce.

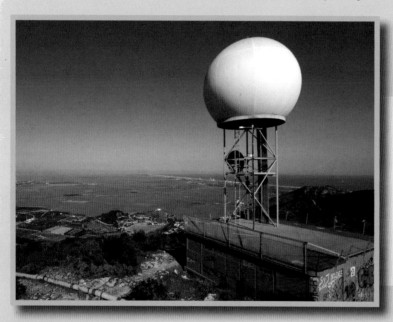

Some weather stations are situated near the coast. Others are located on ships or on islands in the ocean. Meteorologists use information from all the weather stations in the region to build a complete picture.

Weather Stations

Meteorologists also use weather stations all over the world to give them more detailed information about the weather. Instruments measure the direction and speed of the wind, the temperature of the air, and air pressure. When a tropical storm forms, scientists from the National Hurricane Center in Miami, Florida, monitor and track its position across the ocean. They look at changes in the storm's strength as it progresses, and try to forecast where it will make landfall.

Getting Inside the Storm

A hurricane hunter is an airplane that is used as a flying weather station. The pilot flies the aircraft into and out of the storm over and over again, to measure changes in the wind speed. One of the most important measurements is of the air pressure in the eye of the storm.

Most airplanes go out of their way to avoid a hurricane, but not this one! It is one of a squadron of planes that have been equipped to fly right into the center of hurricanes.

WORLD'S FASTEST

On September 25, 1987, Hurricane Emily was moving at 45 miles (72 km) per hour as it crossed the Caribbean island of Bermuda. It then picked up speed and sped northeast over the Atlantic Ocean, reaching nearly 70 miles (112 km) per hour. It was the fastest-moving hurricane of the twentieth century.

This photograph shows the eye of a hurricane taken from a hurricane hunter in the center of it. Instruments on board the plane measure the temperature, humidity, and pressure of the air outside.

HURRICANE WARNING!

The National Hurricane Center warns the public when a hurricane begins to develop. This gives people time to prepare. It is difficult for the center to predict accurately where a storm will make landfall, because hurricanes can suddenly change direction, change speed, or become stronger or weaker. The center can only base their warnings on the information they have so far.

A hurricane gauge shows how high the water could rise for different categories of hurricane. The sign next to it urges people to make a plan of action so that they know what to do should a hurricane strike.

Monitoring Storms

Once the National Hurricane Center is monitoring a tropical storm or hurricane, it issues updates every 6 hours. People watch their televisions to get the latest news. The center issues a hurricane watch for areas that they think may be hit by the hurricane in the next 48 hours. When an area is given a hurricane warning, it means that the center expects the hurricane to strike the area within the next 36 hours.

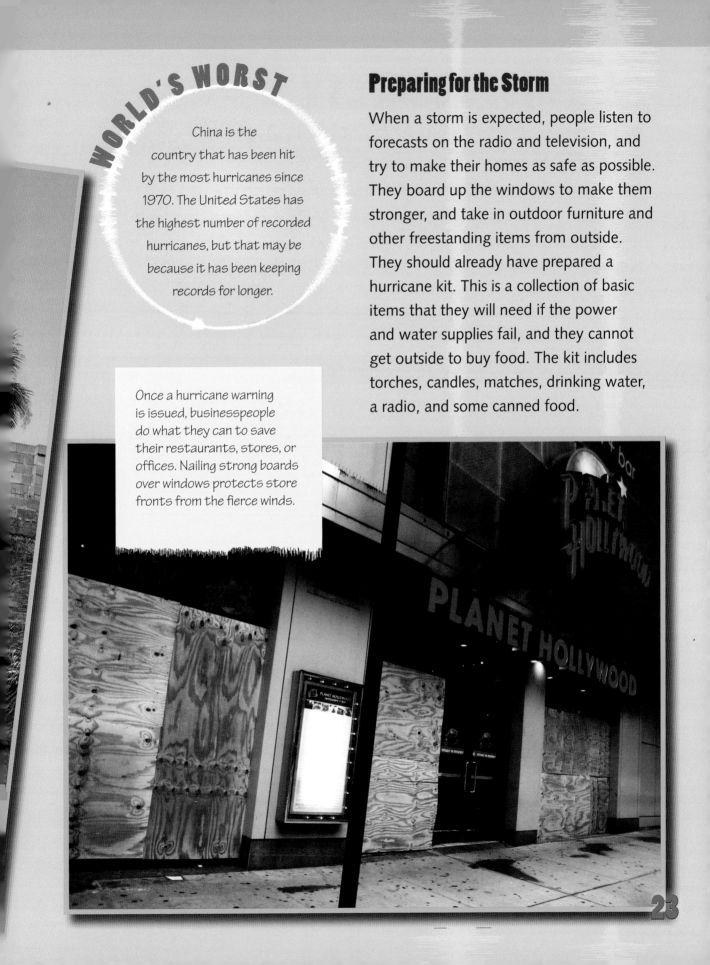

WORLD'S WORST

China is the country that has been hit by the most hurricanes since 1970. The United States has the highest number of recorded hurricanes, but that may be because it has been keeping records for longer.

Preparing for the Storm

When a storm is expected, people listen to forecasts on the radio and television, and try to make their homes as safe as possible. They board up the windows to make them stronger, and take in outdoor furniture and other freestanding items from outside. They should already have prepared a hurricane kit. This is a collection of basic items that they will need if the power and water supplies fail, and they cannot get outside to buy food. The kit includes torches, candles, matches, drinking water, a radio, and some canned food.

Once a hurricane warning is issued, businesspeople do what they can to save their restaurants, stores, or offices. Nailing strong boards over windows protects store fronts from the fierce winds.

23

HEADING FOR SAFETY

When a hurricane watch becomes a hurricane warning, people have to decide whether to stay where they are or travel to somewhere safer. Sometimes they have no choice. People who live near the shore, or in an area likely to flood, may be ordered to evacuate. They then have to leave their homes and drive inland, or go to an evacuation center.

The highways traveling inland from the coast are filled with thousands of cars when a hurricane is expected. Sometimes the lanes in the other direction are also used so that families can get to safety more quickly.

Evacuation Plans

The authorities in areas likely to be hit by hurricanes put together plans to evacuate people in the event of a hurricane. Certain highways are chosen to be evacuation routes. These can get very full when many people want to travel at one time, so plans are put in place to try to avoid this. Evacuation centers are set up in public buildings for people who cannot leave the area. The centers provide shelter until the hurricane is over.

Evacuation routes become jammed with traffic. In 2005, around 2.5 million people drove north from Houston, Texas, before Hurricane Rita arrived. The route was gridlocked for around 100 miles (160 km), trapping people in their cars for up to 48 hours. Many motorists ran out of gas, and had no food or water.

Staying Put

People who are not in immediate danger from flooding often decide to stay in their homes. In addition to the hurricane survival kit, they stock up with food, medicines, and other essentials. Sometimes, people who have lived in a hurricane zone for many years choose not to leave their homes. They have experienced hurricane warnings being issued in the past that were then not followed by a hurricane, because it changed its path. This is a dangerous risk to take. In New Orleans, many people refused to leave their homes as Hurricane Katrina approached in 2005.

In the United States, most people drive to safety from a danger zone. The evacuation routes are very well marked and have been planned in advance by the authorities.

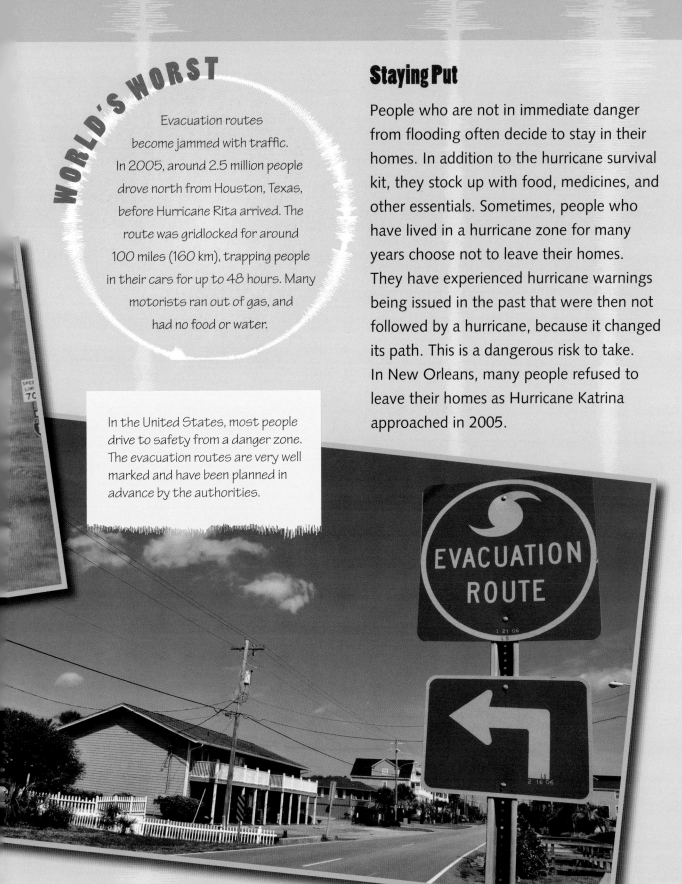

CHAPTER THREE

THE DAMAGE

A hurricane leaves a trail of destruction. Strong winds and heavy floods damage trees, buildings, pylons, and other structures. People may be unable to return to their homes or businesses for weeks, or even years. Damage can be caused to places far from the coast. In 1996, Hurricane Fran swept 150 miles (241 km) inland to hit Raleigh, North Carolina. Thousands of homes were damaged, and there was no power in some areas for several weeks.

Boats in Biloxi, Mississippi, were swept ashore and badly damaged when Hurricane Katrina made landfall.

LAND AND SEA

It is not only people on land who are affected by hurricanes. Fishermen in small boats near the coast are in danger and need to get back into harbor before the storm hits. Large ships either have to take shelter in port or avoid the roughest seas. Aircraft need to avoid hurricanes at all costs. Lightning can damage the instruments on board and make the aircraft crash. Flights do not take off when a hurricane is forecasted.

Counting the Cost

Some people lose everything in a hurricane. Others must spend large sums of money repairing and rebuilding their homes. Government and charity money helps to repair vital services that are needed for the cleanup operation, such as highway and railroad networks and power lines.

WORLD'S WORST

In 2005, Hurricane Katrina became one of the worst ever natural disasters in the United States. It claimed 1,836 lives and caused $81 billion worth of damage, making it the most expensive hurricane ever.

People lived in emergency shelters and makeshift homes after Cyclone Sidr devastated their houses, crops, and land in Bangladesh in 2007. Schools and medical centers were also flattened.

WIND DAMAGE

Hurricanes are categorized by the speed of their winds and by the damage those winds can do. When a strong wind gets under items such as mobile homes and roofs, it can overturn them or blow them away. Strong winds can smash windows, fences, and other fragile structures. The strongest winds can cause very severe damage even to large buildings.

These people returned to their mobile home to rescue some belongings after their trailer was destroyed by Hurricane Irene's devastating winds in 2011.

Type of Wind

Hurricane winds are particularly destructive. They blow strongly for many hours and are turbulent. This means they change speed and direction. Gusts of wind are even stronger than the measured steady speed of the storm. A Category 4 hurricane, for example, with wind speeds of 131 to 155 miles (210 to 249 km) per hour, may have gusts of up to 200 miles (320 km) per hour. As the wind changes direction, it finds any weak points in a structure and damages them.

Flying Missiles

Objects that are smashed and torn from their structures are blown through the air. Advertising signs, tiles, and pieces of wood and plastic become dangerous missiles traveling at high speed. They can injure people and damage buildings. As the storm passes, the debris litters the ground, blocking highways and causing damage.

Skyscrapers are built strongly and designed to withstand hurricane-force winds. Their windows, however, are often smashed or completely blown out. This building was damaged by Hurricane Wilma in 2005.

AUSTRALIA'S WORST

The most destructive cyclone to hit Australia was Cyclone Tracey, which hit the city of Darwin on December 24 and 25, 1974. It killed 71 people. Strong winds and flying debris damaged 90 percent of homes so badly they were uninhabitable. More than 30,000 people were evacuated from the city.

FLOODING

Flooding often accompanies a hurricane when it makes landfall. Flooding is caused by two factors: the hurricane's heavy rain and the storm surge from the ocean. Heavy rainfall causes rivers to spill onto the countryside, towns, and cities. When drains overflow, the water is polluted with sewage, which fills the streets and flows back up pipes into buildings. Seawater from a storm surge pours up the shore. It completely floods the coastal area, and smashes into any buildings in its path.

Bursting its Banks

A large hurricane can mean dozens of inches of rainfall in just a day or two. As rainwater pours into rivers, the water level rises and the river flows faster. Trees and other debris are washed downstream. The force of the deep, rushing water can wash away bridges. When the river bursts its banks, water floods over the land. It destroys crops and threatens livestock. In towns and cities, it pours along streets, washing away vehicles and everything else in its path.

WORLD'S WORST

Cyclone Nina struck China in 1975. It was the most deadly cyclone to hit the Eastern Pacific since 1900. An incredible 64.2 inches (1.6 m) of rain fell along the Banqiao Dam, causing the dam wall to collapse. Another 61 dams also burst. In total, 229,000 people were killed. Of these, 86,000 were killed by the flooding.

Swept Away

Huge waves hit the shore with a massive force. Each wave brings hundreds of tons of fast-moving water. Boats can be swept onto the land, and buildings along the shore smashed by water and debris. If the storm surge happens to coincide with a high tide, the volume and force of the water is even greater. The land along the shore can be very badly eroded.

Automobiles as well as homes are destroyed by floods. The floodwater contains oil, sewage, and dangerous chemicals.

This house once stood near the bank of the river—now it is in the river. When water floods a building, it can weaken its foundations and destroy everything inside it.

31

REAL-LIFE SCIENCE
HURRICANE KATRINA,
New Orleans, 2005

Hurricane Katrina was one of the most devastating hurricanes ever to hit the United States. It brought strong winds and heavy rain. The city of New Orleans, Louisiana, was the worst affected, not so much by the wind or the rain, but by the storm surge. This caused the protective levees that had been built to keep back the sea to fail. As a result, 80 percent of the city was flooded. As the disaster unfolded, local and national governments were accused of failing to protect or help the people of the city.

Americans were shocked by what happened when Hurricane Katrina hit New Orleans. They were even more shocked by what happened next.

New Orleans

The hurricane smashed into New Orleans, the city that took the full force of the storm.

The Path of the Storm

Katrina began over the Caribbean islands of the Bahamas on August 23, 2005. It moved west, over the southern tip of the Florida peninsula and into the Gulf of Mexico. Here it quickly grew more intense, and by August 28 it was a Category 5 hurricane, heading straight for the Gulf Coast. It weakened and made landfall on the southeastern coast of Louisiana as a Category 3 hurricane on August 29. It continued to travel north at the same strength, over New Orleans and through Mississippi.

CANE
NA

floods New Orlean

Survivors Speak

Shilo Groover is a television producer who was in the coastal town of Biloxi when Hurricane Katrina struck there:

"The lights in our studio began pulsating. We rushed to another part of the building and set up makeshift operations, only to hear a crash above us. A piece of concrete had slammed through the roof. Then one of the transmitting towers collapsed. As we were rushing out of our crumbling newsroom the phones were still ringing. The callers were frantic viewers who were stranded in their homes and needed help."

As Katrina made landfall on the southern coast of the United States, its Category 3 winds flattened buildings and scattered debris everywhere.

DEVASTATION

By August 29, around 1 million people had left New Orleans, but more than 100,000 citizens remained. Around 20,000 of these people took shelter in the Superdome. As the storm left the city, everyone breathed a sigh of relief. However, the worst was still to come.

The Unstoppable Ocean

Much of New Orleans is below sea level. Levees are walls built to keep out the water. In 2005, the New Orleans levees were 23 feet (7 m) high, but the storm surge that followed was 28 feet (8.5 m) high. Many floodgates failed, and water up to 20 feet (6 m) deep flooded into the city in 53 different places.

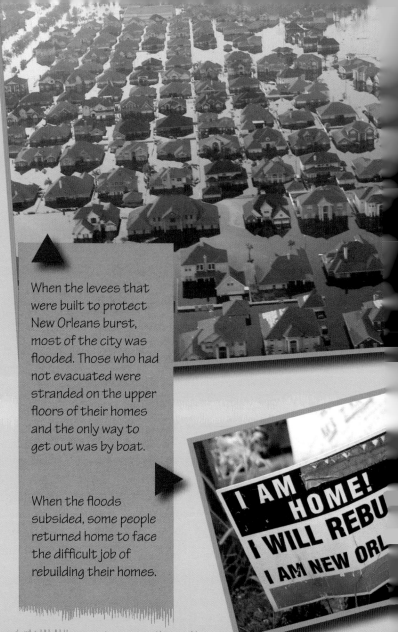

When the levees that were built to protect New Orleans burst, most of the city was flooded. Those who had not evacuated were stranded on the upper floors of their homes and the only way to get out was by boat.

When the floods subsided, some people returned home to face the difficult job of rebuilding their homes.

I AM HOME! I WILL REBU I AM NEW ORL

The Disaster of New Orleans

AUG 23, 2005
Katrina forms as a tropical storm near the Bahamas and moves slowly westward toward Florida. Meteorologists track the progress of the storm as it moves toward land and prepare to issue warnings to people in the southern states.

AUG 25, 2005 6:30 a.m.
Katrina increases to a Category 1 hurricane, before crossing the southern tip of Florida.

AUG 26, 2005
Katrina moves westward over the warm waters of the Gulf of Mexico. As the storm crosses warm water, it very quickly intensifies and gathers speed. The hurricane then begins to move northwest, and then north, heading for the southern states along the coast.

AUG 27, 2005
Katrina strengthens to become a Category 3 storm. The National Hurricane Center issues its first hurricane watch, followed 12 hours later by a hurricane warning for southeast Louisiana through Alabama coasts. People throughout these states are warned to prepare for the hurricane ahead. Some people leave, others decide to ride out the storm instead.

Chaos Erupts

People soon ran out of food and water. Some broke into stores and restaurants to get provisions. The authorities became more worried about crime and looting than about rescuing people. Survivors later reported that they were given no water or food and were prevented from leaving the city.

Many people left their pets at home when they evacuated— they thought they would return in just a few days. This dog has escaped but is desperate and hungry.

Larry and Lorrie were attending a conference for paramedics in New Orleans when they became stranded in the city:

"By day four, our hotels had run out of fuel and water. Street crime as well as water levels began to rise. The hotels turned us out and locked their doors. National Guards told us that the police would not allow us into the Superdome or the Convention Center because they were too chaotic and squalid. We asked, 'If we can't go to the only two shelters in the city, what is our alternative?' The guards told us that that was our problem."

AUG 28, 2005
Katrina strengthens to Category 5, and winds reach 170 miles (274 km) per hour. Katrina weakens to Category 4 and residents from southeast Louisiana through Alabama coasts are told to evacuate. The New Orleans mayor then orders the city to be evacuated. Thousands of people begin to leave the city to try to escape the devastating storm.

AUG 29, 2005 11:10 a.m.
Katrina makes landfall as a Category 3 hurricane at Grand Isle, Louisiana. It moves over Breton Sound and makes landfall again near the border between the states of Louisiana and Mississippi. Then, a storm surge of 25 to 30 feet (7.6 to 9 m) devastates the coasts and floods the cities of Mobile, Biloxi, and Gulfport. The levees in New Orleans are breached and floodwater rushes through the city.

AUG 30, 2005
New Orleans International Airport opens for aircraft to bring aid and rescue personnel.

AUG 31, 2005
Floodwaters in New Orleans continue to rise. Katrina reaches the Great Lakes and moves northeast across Canada.

CHAPTER FOUR
RESCUE AND REBUILD

When a hurricane has passed, the emergency services move in. The first priority is to rescue survivors and to help people who have lost their homes. Many people go to stay with friends and family who live elsewhere, but some are unable to travel, or have nowhere to go. Clearing up the mess and repairing the damage can take months or even years.

The United Nations sent trucks packed with emergency supplies to the survivors of a hurricane in Haiti. Supplies can often take weeks to arrive, because so many people need help and it is difficult to reach isolated areas.

MOST AT RISK

Hurricanes strike some countries much more often than others. China, the United States, and the Philippines are at great risk of being hit by a hurricane. Whatever the country, the poorest people are usually the worst affected. Their homes are often not strongly built, and they cannot afford to protect them well. They have no insurance to rebuild them after a disaster, too. In addition, vulnerable people who are poor, old, or sick are less likely to be able to leave the danger zone and travel to safety.

WORLD'S WORST

Bangladesh is one of the poorest countries in the world. Two huge rivers cross the country and flow into the ocean at the Bay of Bengal. Much of the land is flat and it is often flooded by river water. When a hurricane strikes, islands and land around the river mouths flood. Millions of people lose their homes and their farmland.

Developing countries may be unable to cope with the huge damage caused by hurricanes. International rescue teams often provide support and help in the days following a hurricane disaster.

DVI CH
Disaster Victim Identification
Switzerland

EMERGENCY HELP

When a hurricane strikes, the emergency services are the first to respond. The local authorities may ask for help from both the government and the army. Charities, such as the International Red Cross, are always ready to give money and to send aid workers to help. Organizing all the help is a complex and costly operation.

Immediate Action

The first priority after a disaster is to find survivors and to treat the injured. Floods can trap many people in buildings or under wreckage. They have to be located quickly and, if necessary, dug out. Others will be stranded on rooftops. They have to be rescued by boat or helicopter. Police, firefighters, and local people come to the rescue.

Many survivors of Hurricane Katrina were able to reach dry land around New Orleans and were rescued by army helicopters.

When Cyclone Nargis hit Burma on May 2, 2008, it killed 84,500 people and affected more than 2 million others. Burma's government allowed only a few foreign aid workers into the country. Local Buddhist monks collected and distributed water, rice, and other vital supplies to the survivors. Even the government could not stop them.

Emergency Supplies

Three things are essential for survivors of a natural disaster, such as a hurricane: clean water, food, and shelter. Shelters are set up within a few days, with some supplies of food and water. Getting enough supplies over the coming days can be difficult. Flooded and damaged highways hamper the efforts of any supply trucks trying to reach the most devastated areas. Supplies often have to be flown in by plane or helicopter. Many people are needed to set up tents and temporary shelters, distribute the aid, and look after the survivors.

Rescue teams move quickly across water to search for and help people trapped by hurricane flooding.

REAL-LIFE SCIENCE
HAITI, 2008

In 2008, the small country of Haiti, located in the Caribbean between Cuba and Puerto Rico, was battered by four devastating storms in just three weeks. Tropical storm Fay came first, on August 18. It was followed by three hurricanes: Gustav, Hanna, and Ike. By September 8, nine out of Haiti's ten regional departments were flooded. More than 800 people were killed and 1 million people lost their homes. Everything in the country was badly affected. Farmland was damaged or destroyed, many highways and bridges disappeared, and homes, schools, and hospitals were destroyed.

The city of Gonaïves, Haiti, was all but destroyed by the devastating hurricanes of 2008. Many people there were forced to leave forever.

Gonaïves

Huge waves crashed onto the shore during Hurricane Ike. In Haiti, they caused devastating flooding in villages along the coast.

Lionel and his wife were at home in Gonaïves when hurricane Hanna struck the island:

"At about 11:00 p.m., the water started rising. As it began to spread under the bed, we knew we had to move. We managed to get onto the roof of one of the highest houses in the area. We watched as the street disappeared under the rising water. We spent 5 days up there, along with 25 other people, with no food or water. We have lost everything."

Children had to walk through streets of mud to get to their homes in Gonaïves, Haiti. Even weeks after Hurricane Ike, the ground in much of Haiti was saturated.

Flooding and Mudslides

When Hurricane Gustav arrived a week after Fay, the torrential rain fell onto ground that was already wet. The water created flash floods that in turn created giant mudslides. Torrents of mud poured down the mountainsides, sweeping trees and crops away and flooding into people's homes. As their houses filled with mud, people took shelter on the rooftops. Before Haitians could begin to recover, Hurricanes Hanna and Ike added yet more rain and chaos.

Gonaïves Destroyed

The city of Gonaïves in the north of the country was particularly badly hit. When the River Quinte burst its banks, it destroyed 80 percent of the city. Both the city and the farmland around it were covered with water, mud, and debris. Hurricane Ike destroyed the last remaining bridge in the city.

41

AFTER THE STORMS

When aid workers and other helpers arrived in Haiti after Hurricane Ike had struck the island, they found a devastated country. People were stranded on rooftops surrounded by deep, muddy water. The cities of Gonaïves, Cabaret, Hinche, and Jacmel were the worst affected. Aid workers found it difficult to reach survivors because bridges had been destroyed and many highways blocked by landslides.

The work to clear up the mud left by the floods began immediately. It took months before many people were able to return to their homes.

Immediate Action

The first task for rescuers was to distribute emergency packages, which contained food and water purification tablets. It took several days for the floodwater to drain away. When survivors did return to their homes, they found they were uninhabitable. In Gonaïves, most of the 350,000 residents were homeless.

The Trail of Disaster

AUG 18, 2008
Tropical Storm Fay drops heavy rain on Haiti, causing sudden floods.

AUG 26, 2008
Hurricane Gustav forms around 260 miles (418 km) southeast of Haiti and then quickly strengthens to then become a hurricane.

AUG 26, 2008
1:00 p.m.
Gustav makes landfall on Haiti near the town of Jacmel, with winds of 75 miles (121 km) per hour. Heavy rain causes flooding and mudslides.

AUG 27, 2008
Gustav moves across the city of Gonaïves in the north and

back over the ocean. Gustav kills five Haitians and leaves around 7,000 more people homeless.

AUG 28–SEP 4, 2008
Gustav strikes Jamaica and then strengthens from a Category 3 to a Category 4 hurricane before crossing Cuba. The hurricane ravages

the island before it continues north across the Gulf of Mexico to make landfall on Louisiana.

AUG 28, 2008
Hurricane Hanna forms as a tropical storm near the Leeward Islands.

SEP 1, 2008
Hanna strengthens as it moves close to

Rolande Jean and her family lived in the small coastal town of Nippes in Haiti:

"When Hurricane Ike roared ashore, our home was directly in its path. As we huddled inside the house, the water flooded in and the roof was torn off. We were in despair, but help arrived. The charity Caritas gave us 20 sacks of concrete and 40 roofing sheets. They paid for laborers, and we helped rebuild the house as well. Until the charity came, we had no help at all."

Ordinary people in Gonaïves helped to distribute cooking oil and other supplies provided by the United States.

Children and their families took refuge in a church compound in Gonaïves. Here they received food and clean clothes while waiting to return to their homes.

Over a Month Later

Five weeks later, on October 13, Gonaïves still had no water, electricity, and other essential services. Thousands of homeless people either had to move in with friends and neighbors, or make a temporary home in tents and huts provided by charities and other organizations. Much still had to be done to help Haitians get back on their feet.

the Bahamas, and becomes a Category 1 hurricane. Hanna weakens to a tropical storm, but causes heavy rain on Haiti. Floods in Gonaïves cause catastrophic damage, killing around 500 people and also leaving around 50,000 others homeless.

SEP 5–7, 2008
Hanna makes landfall on South Carolina, and then moves up the East Coast of the United States.

SEP 3, 2008
Tropical storm Ike takes just 12 hours to suddenly strengthen to a violent Category 4 hurricane.

SEP 5, 2008
Winds devastate 80 percent of buildings on Grand Turk Island. Much of the island is left in complete devastation by the hurricane's force.

SEP 7, 2008
The outer edge of Ike causes mass flooding in Haiti, killing more than 74 Haitians. The flooding also destroys

the only remaining bridge in Gonaïves. The city is left in ruins.

SEP 8–14, 2008
Ike makes landfall on Cuba, before crossing the Gulf of Mexico. It makes landfall as a Category 2 hurricane on Galveston Island, Texas, and then continues through the Midwest to Pennsylvania.

REBUILDING AFTER DISASTER

Restoring the buildings, services, and homes in a hurricane zone can take several years. Repairing electricity and water supplies can be done in days, but often takes longer if the affected areas are remote or inaccessible. Repairing highways and rebuilding bridges may take months. Rebuilding people's homes and providing everything they need to start normal life again can go on for many years.

Residents of New Orleans began to repair their homes after Hurricane Katrina. Many wore masks to avoid breathing in harmful bacteria and poison from the rotting debris.

Better Building

Before rebuilding begins, authorities need to consider what measures they can take to help prevent future hurricanes causing such extensive damage. For example, levees and floodwalls can be built much higher and stronger to withstand a storm surge. New building techniques can be used to minimize the damage caused by a hurricane.

WORLD'S WORST

Floodwaters in New Orleans became a poisonous mixture of chemicals, sewage, metals, and oil. As the water drained away, the poisons soaked through the ground and polluted groundwater across hundreds of miles of land.

Who Pays?

Local, state, and central governments usually pay for repairs to highways, bridges, floodwalls, and public buildings. Many people insure their homes or businesses against hurricane and flood damage. They pay a sum of money to the insurance company every month, and the company pays for the repairs if they become necessary. Insurance, however, costs a lot of money and many people cannot afford it. These are the people who may lose most when a hurricane strikes.

The Poorest Countries

The poorest countries face the toughest road to recovery after a hurricane. In Honduras in October 1998, Hurricane Mitch left the country totally devastated. Floods, mudslides, and winds wrecked crops and destroyed towns and villages across the country. Thousands of people died, and many thousands more lost their means of making a living when the agricultural land was destroyed. One of the poorest nations on Earth needed to locate billions of dollars to get it back on its feet.

Engineers worked hard to repair power lines damaged by Hurricane Irene. It took several weeks for all residents to have their electricity restored.

GLOSSARY

air pressure: the force of air as it presses on the surface of objects

debris: the remains of something broken down or destroyed

delta: the area where a river widens as it reaches the ocean

evacuate: to leave a dangerous place

flash flood: a sudden flood caused by very heavy rain

floodgate: a gate that keeps out the flow of a large amount of water

gridlock: a traffic jam that is so bad no vehicle can move in any direction

high tide: when the level of the sea is at its highest on the shore

insurance: a contract in which a person pays a sum of money to a company and the company pays for any losses due, for example, those caused by a hurricane

landslide: when part of a hill or mountainside slides downhill

levee: a high bank or wall built along a river, lake, or the shore to stop water flooding onto the land

meteorologist: a scientist who studies the weather

monitor: to watch over a period of time

mudslide: a thick mixture of soil and water that slides rapidly downhill

transmitting tower: a mast that carries equipment to transmit signals, such as radio and television signals

tropical: connected to the warm areas of Earth on each side of the equator, between the Tropic of Cancer and the Tropic of Capricorn

turbulent: chaotic, constantly changing speed and direction

water purification: the killing of germs in water so that it is safe to drink

weather station: an observation post with instruments for recording and measuring aspects of the weather

FOR MORE INFORMATION

Books

Royston, Angela. *Hurricanes.* New York, NY: Marshall Cavendish Benchmark, 2011.

Simon, Seymour. *Hurricanes*. New York: Harper Collins, 2007.

Sheets, Bob and Jack Williams. *Hurricane Watch: Forecasting the Deadliest Storms on Earth*. New York, NY: Vintage, 2001.

Tarshis, Lauren. *I Survived Hurricane Katrina, 2005*. New York, NY: Scholastic, 2011.

Websites

Find lots of information about how hurricanes form, and personal stories about living through them.
www.eo.ucar.edu/webweather/hurricanehome.html

The agency for preparing for, protecting against, and recovering from disasters is FEMA. Their website has excellent information on hurricanes.
www.ready.gov/hurricanes

This website has all you need to know about how hurricanes happen and how to stay safe when they hit.
www.weatherwizkids.com/weather-hurricane.htm

INDEX